COOKING THROUGHOUT AMERICAN HISTORY™

What Was Cooking in Edith Roosevelt's White House?

Tanya Larkin

The Rosen Publishing Group's
PowerKids Press™
New York

The recipes in this cookbook are intended for a child to make together with an adult.

Many thanks to Ruth Rosen and her test kitchen.

Published in 2001 by The Rosen Publishing Group, Inc.
29 East 21st Street, New York, NY 10010

First Edition

Book Design: Danielle Primiceri
Layout Design: Emily Muschinske

Photo Credits: pp. 4, 9, 12, 15, 19 © Bettmann/CORBIS; pp. 7, 11, 17, 21 © Dean Galiano.
Prop: Teddy bear, p. 17, created by Frances I. Ruffin,

Larkin, Tanya.
       What was cooking in Edith Roosevelt's White House? / Tanya Larkin.
          p. cm.— (Cooking throughout American history)
       Includes index.
       Summary: This book describes Edith Kermit Roosevelt, wife of the 26th president of the United States, her role as first lady, and some of the foods she served at various stages of her life. Includes recipes.
       ISBN 0-8239-5611-3
       1. Cookery, American—Juvenile literature. 2. Roosevelt, Edith Kermit Carow, 1861–1948—Juvenile literature. [1. Roosevelt, Edith Kermit Carow, 1861–1948. 2. First ladies. 3. Women—Biography. 4. Cookery, American.] I. Title. II. Series.
       2000
       641.3'00973—dc21

Manufactured in the United States of America

Contents

4

The Accidental First Couple

In 1901, Theodore and Edith Roosevelt unexpectedly became the 26th president and first lady of the United States. Theodore was vice president when President William McKinley was shot and killed. Theodore was required to take the president's place. Although the American public **mourned** President McKinley's death, they welcomed their new president. Theodore Roosevelt was already an American hero. During the Spanish-American War, Theodore had led a group of special soldiers called the "Rough Riders" to capture American-owned land in Cuba. The American public gladly received Theodore and Edith into the White House. Their young, large family also brightened the mood of the White House.

◄ *Theodore and Edith Roosevelt were the 26th president and first lady of the United States. Theodore is shown here with a grandson.*

A Young Family

Edith Kermit and Theodore Roosevelt were friends from childhood. Theodore married Edith in 1886, two years after the death of his first wife. His daughter Alice was 17 when the family moved into the White House. Alice was Theodore's daughter from his first marriage. The other children were Ted, 14, Kermit, 12, Ethel, 10, Archie, 7, and Quentin, 4. The Roosevelt children were called "TR's brood" and the "White House Gang." Edith used to joke that the president was her "oldest and worst child." He liked to join in the children's pillow fights and tell bedtime stories or ghost stories in the dark. The Roosevelt children also loved eating treats. Edith had the family cook prepare cookies called sugar wafers. They were Alice's favorite. Alice enjoyed them so much, that many years later, she served them to guests who came to her home for tea.

Sugar Wafers

You will need:

For orange wafers:
½ cup (118 ml) soft butter
¾ cup (177 ml) sugar
1 egg
1 teaspoon (5 ml) grated
    orange rind
1 tablespoon (15 ml) fresh
    orange juice
1½ cups (355 ml) flour
½ teaspoon (2.5 ml) baking
    powder
¼ teaspoon (1.2 ml) salt

For chocolate wafers:
Add 3 tablespoons (44 ml) of
cocoa powder to the flour.

HOW TO DO IT:

☞ Have an adult help you heat oven to 375 degrees Fahrenheit (191° C).
☞ Beat butter and sugar together.
☞ Add egg and beat until light and fluffy.
☞ Add remaining ingredients. Mix well.
☞ Drop a level teaspoonful (5 ml) of dough, or a rounded teaspoonful (for larger cookies), onto an ungreased cookie sheet.
☞ Press each cookie flat with a butter knife, or with cheesecloth dampened with cold water.
☞ Bake for about 7 minutes.
☞ When done, edges of cookies are slightly brown. Remove from cookie sheet immediately.
☞ Makes about 3 dozen cookies.

Sagamore Hill

Before Edith and her family moved to Washington, D. C., in 1902, they spent a lot of time at Sagamore Hill, the Roosevelt family home on Long Island, New York. Theodore was an outdoorsman, a **conservationist**, and a hunter. His hunting **trophies** hung from the walls. A **cabinet member** visiting from Washington might look up during a discussion to find a moose head staring back at him. Theodore was given the nickname "Teddy" by the **press**. When he refused to shoot a sick bear while on a hunting trip in 1903, people began to call stuffed toy bears "teddy bears." At Sagamore Hill, Theodore liked to take his children on long hikes called "tramps." Edith loved her home at Sagamore Hill. As her children grew up and moved away, Edith once remarked that, "They have all gone away from the house on the hill."

Theodore Roosevelt was a hunter. Many of the things he hunted appeared in his "trophy room" at Sagamore Hill. ▶

An Easygoing House

The Roosevelts brought the same dining habits that they had at Sagamore Hill to the White House. One of Edith's most treasured recipes was for biscuits filled with currants, called "fat rascals." These biscuits were served for breakfast with hard-boiled eggs. The Roosevelt children swore that their father drank a bathtub full of coffee to wash his breakfast down. Lunch was usually informal and relaxed. When last-minute guests appeared for lunch, Edith Roosevelt had her kitchen staff serve them leftovers from the night before that might include cantaloupe, freshly baked bread, and tea. Edith was known as a calm and organized woman. She was the first president's wife to employ a social secretary in the White House. This person was hired to organize the social events that Edith held and attended.

Currant-Filled Biscuits

You will need:

2 cups (473 ml) sifted
   flour
2½ teaspoons (12.3 ml)
   baking powder
1 teaspoon (5 ml) salt
⅓ cup (79 ml) shortening
⅔ cup (158 ml) milk
½ cup (118 ml) currants
Butter
Jam

HOW TO DO IT:

☞ Have an adult help you preheat the oven to 425
   degrees Fahrenheit (128° C).

☞ Sift together flour, baking powder and salt in a
   mixing bowl.

☞ Add currants.

☞ Add shortening by mixing flour with two butter
   knives. The mixture should look like very
   small pebbles.

☞ Slowly add the milk until it is soft, not sticky.

☞ Pour dough onto a floured surface.

☞ Roll or pat dough until it is ½ inch (1.3 cm) thick.

☞ Cut out dough with a biscuit or cookie cutter.

☞ Place on an ungreased cookie sheet. Bake 12 to
   15 minutes until brown.

☞ Serve with butter and jam. Makes about 16 biscuits.

A Family Circus

The Roosevelt children played in every corner of the newly decorated White House. When she moved into the White House, Edith got rid of the dark, unattractive, old-fashioned furniture there. She also asked Congress for money to expand and **modernize** the house. She allowed her young children to roller skate down the corridors and to walk around the house on stilts. Visitors found not only children everywhere, but also a zoo full of pets. Kermit's kangaroo rat often came to the breakfast table for lumps of sugar. Quentin, the most **mischievous** Roosevelt, snuck his pony named Algonquin into a White House elevator to take up to his sick brother Archie's room. Seeing the pony made Archie feel better. Quentin liked to carry around a green snake named Emily Spinach.

◀ *Edith Roosevelt, sitting at the far right, and her family enjoyed outdoor adventures and picnics.*

Princess Alice

Alice was Theodore Roosevelt's daughter from his first marriage, to Alice Lee. Young Alice Roosevelt was a **witty** girl and she also liked to play **pranks**. She kept a garter snake in her purse to shock others. She loved to dress in beautiful clothes, and she drove around in her own car. The press nicknamed her "Princess Alice" and reported her every move in the newspapers. In 1906, Alice married a **politician**, Nicholas Longworth. Edith organized the wedding. She had a 130-pound (59 ml) wedding cake made. It was decorated with orange blossoms and sugar doves. Alice grew impatient while cutting the wedding cake for guests. She borrowed a sword from a military aide to finish cutting the cake.

Alice Roosevelt was a beautiful bride when she married Nicholas Longworth in 1906. She is photographed here with her husband on the left and her father Theodore on the right. ▶

Winter and Summer Treats

Alice Roosevelt Longworth died in 1980. She had written a lot of **memoirs** about her family's time in the White House. She especially remembered the joyful mood inspired by snowy days. Washington, D.C., usually has mild winters, so snowstorms are a shocking surprise. If there was more than six inches (15.2 cm) of snow, the Roosevelt children celebrated. That meant they could make "snow ice cream" outside. It was a cooling refreshment after hours of sledding. The children dug into the stiff snow with spoons and piled it into buckets. They poured custard over the fresh snow while they were still outside. Another favorite cool treat, probably served in the summer, was a frozen mixture of lemons, sugar, and milk.

Lemon-Flavored Milk Ice

Juice of 3 lemons
2 cups (473 ml) of sugar
1 quart (946 ml) of milk
Lemon slices
Mint (optional)

HOW TO DO IT:

☞ Blend lemon juice and sugar and let stand for six hours.

☞ Add milk to the lemon-sugar mixture. Pour into a plastic bowl and place in the freezer. When frozen, scrape into dessert bowls or mugs. Top with lemon slices and mint.

☞ Serves 4 to 6.

A cup of lemon-flavored milk ice was a delicious way that the Roosevelt children got their milk. It can also be a cool treat during the summer.

Roosevelt Holidays

The Roosevelts looked forward to all special holidays at the White House and their summers at Sagamore Hill. For the family's Thanksgivings, Edith Roosevelt had White House chefs prepare a roast pig with an apple in its mouth, turkey, southern-style sugared sweet potatoes, and ice cream in the shape of birds with "sugar gravy" poured over them. Every Christmas Eve, Edith filled the children's stockings with gifts. On Christmas morning, the children would burst into their parents' bedroom and look at their stocking gifts. Theodore insisted that they wait until after breakfast to open their bigger gifts in the library. The Roosevelts' Christmas was like many other American families. In fact, the Roosevelts were the first family to have a Christmas tree in the White House.

The photo shows, from the left, Quentin, President Roosevelt, Ted, Archie, Alice, Kermit, ▶
Mrs. Roosevelt, and Ethel. This photo was taken at their home in Sagamore Hill.

A Stag Dinner

Edith Roosevelt was a talented **hostess**. She gave special luncheons for the wives of cabinet members. She also entertained artists and important **intellectuals** of the time. When Edith gave parties for the wives of cabinet members, each woman was given a **bouquet** of flowers that matched her dress. Edith was not invited to her most successful party, however. It was a **stag dinner** for Prince Henry of Prussia. No women were invited. She planned a 10-course menu that was written in French. The men ate turtle, beef, and duck, among other **exotic** dishes. Edith knew that Prince Henry enjoyed sailing. Edith had the East Room of the White House decorated with symbols having to do with ships. She also placed tiny German and American flags in the dessert.

Senegalese Soup

You will need:

½ cup (118 ml) onion, finely chopped

¼ cup (59 ml) carrot, finely chopped

¼ cup (59 ml) celery, finely chopped

1 small apple, cored, peeled, chopped

2½ cups (591 ml) canned chicken stock

1 tablespoon (15 ml) curry powder

1½ tablespoons (22 ml) flour

1 pinch chili powder

1 teaspoon (5 ml) salt

1 jar strained peas, baby food

1½ cups (354 ml) heavy cream

chopped green onions

HOW TO DO IT:

☞ Simmer onion, carrot, celery, and apple in chicken stock in a large saucepan until tender.

☞ Add curry powder, flour, chili powder, salt, and peas.

☞ Cool for 15 minutes.

☞ Have an adult help you pour the mixture into a blender. Puree.

☞ Pour into a large bowl and place in refrigerator.

☞ When chilled, serve with chopped green onions. Serves four.

The Roosevelts liked bringing back recipes found during their travels to faraway lands. One such recipe was Senegalese soup.

21

Full Final Years

In 1904, Theodore Roosevelt won the presidency in a **landslide** victory. Edith was proud that her husband was elected for a second term. During his years in the White House, Theodore Roosevelt was an energetic leader. Edith's calm manner provided a balance for her husband's childlike excitement. In 1909, after serving four more years, the Roosevelts left the White House. To celebrate their return to private life, they went on a **safari** in Africa. In 1919, Theodore Roosevelt died of a heart attack at the age of 60. Edith lived for many years after his death. She enjoyed reading and traveling. She also devoted much of her time to charity work. Before Edith Roosevelt died at the age of 87, she told a friend that she would like her gravestone to read, "Everything she did was for the happiness of others."

Glossary

bouquet (BOO-kay) An attractive bunch of flowers that are tied together.

cabinet member (KAB-nit MEM-bur) A person who acts as an adviser to a president or other important government official.

conservationist (kon-ser-VAY-shun-ist) Someone who wants to protect nature.

exotic (iks-ZAH-tik) Things that are foreign or unusual.

hostess (HOS-tes) A woman who gives a party and invites guests.

intellectuals (in-tel-EK-cheh-welz) Well-educated, smart people.

landslide (LAND-slyd) A huge number of votes during an election.

memoirs (MEM-wahrz) Books or letters about personal experiences.

mischievous (MIS-chuh-vis) To be playful, sometimes to get into trouble.

modernize (MAH-der-nyz) To bring up-to-date.

mourned (MORND) Felt or expressed grief or sorrow.

politician (pah-lih-TIH-shun) A person who holds or runs for a public office.

pranks (PRAANKS) Playing tricks on someone.

press (PRES) News reporters, publishers, and broadcasters.

safari (suh-FAHR-ee) A journey through Africa to see the land and animals.

stag dinner (STAG DIH-ner) A dinner or party attended only by men.

trophies (TROH-feez) Things gained or given in victory, or mounted as a memorial.

witty (WIT-ee) To be clever, intelligent, and amusing.

Index

Web Sites

To learn more about Edith Roosevelt, check out these Web sites:
http://www.theodoreroosevelt.org/life/familytree/Edith.htm
http://www.theodoreroosevelt.org/kidscorner/trchildrens.htm
http://www.whitehouse.gov/WH/glimpse/presidents/html/tr26.html

J
641.3
LAR

OCT 2000

Larkin, Tanya
What was cooking in Edith
Roosevelt's White House?